The Bat

The Bat

BY NINA LEEN

HOLT RINEHART and WINSTON · NEW YORK

Printed in the United States of America
Layout by Nina Leen
10 9 8 7 6 5 4 3 2

Library of Congress Cataloging in Publication Data
Leen, Nina, date
   The bat.

   SUMMARY: Text and photographs present some unusual characteristics of the life of this elusive and
often misunderstood mammal.
   1. Bats—Juvenile literature.   [1. Bats]
I. Title.
QL737.C5L43   599'.4   75–32252
ISBN 0–03–015581–9

The Bat

Some time ago, Miriam Chaikin, an editor at Holt, Rinehart and Winston, suggested that I do a book on bats for "beginners," people who know little or nothing about bats. The first "reluctant beginner" turned out to be the editor herself. She wasn't crazy about bats—to put it mildly. I was curious how our work would progress, but after weeks of looking at bat pictures and reading about them, she started to show signs of "expertise" in bat matters. If my fears disappeared and Miriam Chaikin could overcome her aversion there is hope for the most reluctant beginner.

I would like to thank Dr. Karl Koopman for writing the Preface and bringing the "Bats in This Book" list up to date. Also my thanks to Arthur M. Greenhall, research associate, Smithsonian Institution, and Elizabeth Greenhall for all the help they gave me. Everybody in Time Inc. Lab was very helpful; without them I could not have done it.

N. L.

TABLE OF CONTENTS

PREFACE

Bats, the only truly flying mammals, form a major group, generally called an order, of more than eight hundred species. The name of this order is Chiroptera, a word of Greek origin meaning "hand wing." Though many people think that bats are pretty much alike, this is far from true. Perhaps it is because most kinds of bats are confined to the tropics and almost all are nocturnal that they are so poorly known to most people. Few bats have any common names. The "common" names are not understood universally. They have all been made up by commentators or writers who felt the need to name a species. Therefore, those scientists who study bats usually use scientific names of Latin or Greek origin which are internationally recognized. This greatly facilitates exchange of information about this fascinating species.

Actually, most bats are poorly understood even by the scientists who work with them. Surprises are to be expected even in basic systematic knowledge, as was evident when a few years ago a new family of bats was discovered. Certainly when it comes to knowledge about geographical distribution, food habits, roosting sites, and many other basic facts of natural history, a great deal is still to be learned. Judging by the diversity among bats for which information on these matters is already available, new information should be fascinating indeed.

One of the many peculiar characteristics of bats is the matter of longevity. Most small mammals of shrew or mouse size live only a year, or two at most, under natural conditions. Many bats of equally small size, however, live for at least ten years and there are records of bats reaching ages of twenty years or more. Such longevity is otherwise known only for animals of much larger size. At least a partial explanation for this may lie in the characteristic of heterothermy—the ability to regulate body temperatures under certain conditions. Bats maintain high body temperatures while in flight but can lower their metabolism while inactive in the roost. Many living in cold climates hibernate for several months each year. The really active period in many bats may actually last for an hour or two each night.

Available bat "housing" is limited and needs safeguarding. Certain bats require specific roosting places. Others require yet other conditions for hibernation and rearing of the young. Only a limited number of caves provide the temperature and humidity for hibernation or for raising the young of a certain species. The survival of that species may well be endangered if the conditions of such a cave are modified. Modification may be caused by physical alteration of a cave; by commercilization, such as heavy human visitor use involving flashlights, and torches; and by other physical disturbances which would affect babies after birth or toward the end of hibernation when energy reserves are low. While such factors as pesticides may affect bats, bat conservation is primarily directed toward conservation of bat roosting places.

KARL F. KOOPMAN
Associate Curator
The American Museum of Natural History

BATS FEATURED IN THIS BOOK

	COMMON NAME	LATIN NAME	RANGE	PAGE
1.	Dog-faced bat	Rousettus aegyptiacus	Africa, Southwestern Asia	17, 22, 28
2.	Flying fox bat	Pteropus giganteus	India	27, 29, 38, 32, 59, 62, 63, 66, 67
3.	African epaulette bat	Epomophorus Sp.	Central Africa	61
4.	Short-nosed fruit bat	Cynopterus brachyotus	Southeast Asia	16, 26, 27
5.	Mouse-tailed bat	Rhinopoma microphyllum	Northern Africa, Southern Asia	15
6.	Giant African leaf-nosed bat	Hipposideros commersoni gigas	West Africa	19, 24, 34, 39, 64, 65, 67
7.	Fishing bulldog bat	Noctilio leporinus	Mexico, Central and South America, West Indies	20, 54, 55
8.	Greater mustache bat	Pteronotus parnellii	Mexico, Central and South America, West Indies	58
9.	Big-eared bat	Macrotus californicus	Northwestern Mexico, South-western United States	23, 28, 31, 35, 39, 50-53
10.	False vampire bat	Vampyrum spectrum	Central and South America	57
11.	Jamaican nectar-feeder bat	Monophyllus redmani redmani	Jamaica	29
12.	Nectar-feeder bat	Leptonycteris sanborni	Mexico, Southwest USA	40, 41, 42, 43, 44, 45

13.	Yellow-shouldered bat	Sturnira Sp.	Central and South America, Mexico, and Lesser Antilles	60
14.	Jamaican flower bat	Phyllonycteris aphylla	Jamaica	20, 48, 49, 60
15.	Vampire bat	Desmodus rotundus	Mexico, Central and South America	32, 36, 37, 56
16.	Hoary bat	Lasiurus cinereus cinereus	North America	76, 77
17.	Lump-nosed bat	Plecotus Townsendii	United States, Canada, Mexico	18, 25
18.	Spotted bat	Euderma maculatum	Western United States, Northwestern Mexico	72, 73, 74, 75
19.	Pallid bat	Antrozous pallidus	Western United States, Mexico	17, 39
20.	Mexican free-tailed guano bat	Tadarida brasiliensis mexicana	Southern and Western United States, Mexico	38, 68, 69, 70, 71
21.	Big free-tailed bat	Tadarida macrotis	Southwestern United States, Mexico, Central and South America	26, 33
22.	Velvety free-tailed bat	Molossus ater nigricans	Mexico, Central America	21

FOREWORD

There is no other living
mammal like it!

Some years ago, whenever I saw a bat I screamed. Millions of people
scream when they see bats, so I assumed it was a natural reaction. I expected
an unprovoked attack with indescribable consequences.

A blind belief that a bat is a vicious creature is deeply rooted in the minds
of most people. Vampire movies showing a giant bat with a six-foot
wingspan (usually a mechanical contraption) landing on a bedroom balcony
in search of blood give a wrong image to the small, shy vampire. Vampire
bats are never found in castles of Transylvania or anywhere else in Europe.
They are strictly New World bats, living in warm regions south of the
Mexican border.

Although no blood-drinking bats live in the United States, many rational
people claim to have seen vampires in their back yards. When a bat chasing
an insect flies around a porch or enters a room, everybody panics. "Kill the
bat!" is the family battle cry. Armed with brooms and sticks, grown men
and women hit the "devilish" little animal till it is dead. This is not necessary—
the bat would have left if given a chance.

I can't blame myself and others for acting irrationally—we did not know
better. Nobody told us. The few books about bats were written by scientists.
Only they were interested in bats. The average person got his information
from reading strange stories and seeing sinister movies designed only to
thrill and frighten them.

My attitude changed when I was assigned to photograph Dr. Donald
R. Griffin working with fishing bats at the Tropical Research Station in
Trinidad and I met, face to face, a bright orange bat with silvery wings. I
never expected to see a colorful animal flying gracefully over water. I
always thought bats were dark creatures with black wings, grotesque faces,
and unpredictable behavior. I was never more wrong.

I have now become used to the idea that it is *me* telling people "There is nothing wrong with bats! They are furry, little animals with wings—that's all." But to say "that's all" is a gross understatement.

Everything I learned about bats was unusual and fascinating. Bats are the largest mammalian population on earth after rodents. And they are the only mammals with wings, able to fly high or low, long and far. Except for insects and birds, no other animal has the power of flight. Bats share with humans an ancient ancestor—the shrew—and anatomically they can be compared to Primates. They possess intelligence and they are capable of learning.

Bats are good examples of "exceptions to rules." Most of them do live in caves. But many roost in trees, in towers, under bridges, in country barns and city houses. Most of them do roost hanging upside down, but others sleep resting on flat rocks or roost in rock crevices, heads up. The majority of bats do fly only by night. But some species start flying before sundown and there are bats known to fly during the day. Maybe this is one of the reasons why they are difficult to find and classify—they are independent and they break the rules.

Nature did not provide humans with the many complex advantages it gave bats. People are not born with wings to fly. Nor can they emit through nose or mouth ultrasonic cries for echolocation, to find their way in the dark. And they cannot, at will, radically reduce or reactivate body energy in minutes' time. Bats can do this for hours or days—when the weather is bad and the food supply is low. (Does it sound similar to Eastern meditation techniques now practiced in the West?) Those are only a few of the things bats can do and people cannot. There are many more marvels scientists try to learn from bats in order to make humans and their world more perfect.

Bats are not eager to meet people. They will hardly profit from close contact with their civilized neighbors. But people could gain fascinating knowledge about those unique mammals if they would only forget the unfounded suspicions and take an objective look at an animal whose only crime is to be able to fly in the dark.

There are cultures and countries where the bat is not considered "evil." In China the word for the bat is *Fu*—the same word means "happiness" or "good luck." Two bats pictured on the cover of a gift mean good wishes from the donor. The design of a tree surrounded by five bats is a symbol of happiness, health, wealth, long life, and tranquility. Maybe the ancient civilizations knew more about bats than we do.

Not everybody in the West is against bats. Noted scientists plead their case and try to save them from destruction. Several European countries have laws to protect them, and if people will listen, the senseless tortures and killings may stop. This planet belongs to everybody—including bats.

N. L.

Anatomy of a Bat

Old drawing of the mouse-tailed bat, *Rhinopoma microphyllum*, explains why, for thousands of years, people have described the bat as a bird, a mouse, or nearly human.

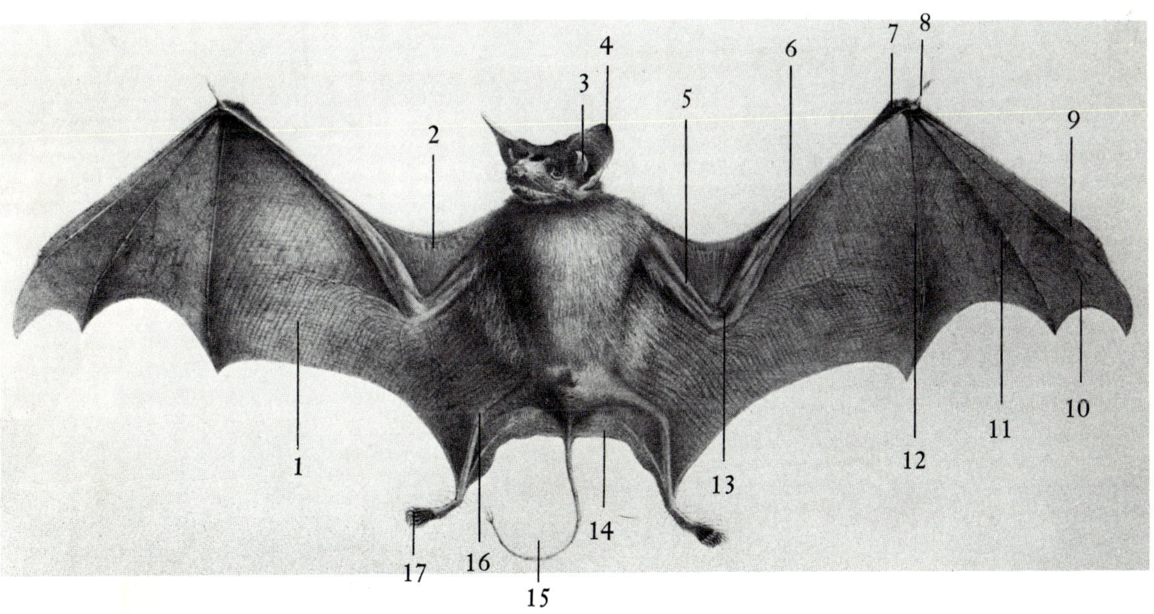

1. Wing membrane	8. Thumb
2. Antebrachial membrane	9. Second finger
3. Tragus	10. Third finger
4. Ear	11. fourth finger
5. Upper arm	12. Fifth finger
6. Forearm	13. Elbow
7. Wrist	14. Interfemoral membrane
	15. Tail
	16. Knee
	17. Foot

Not all Bats Look Alike

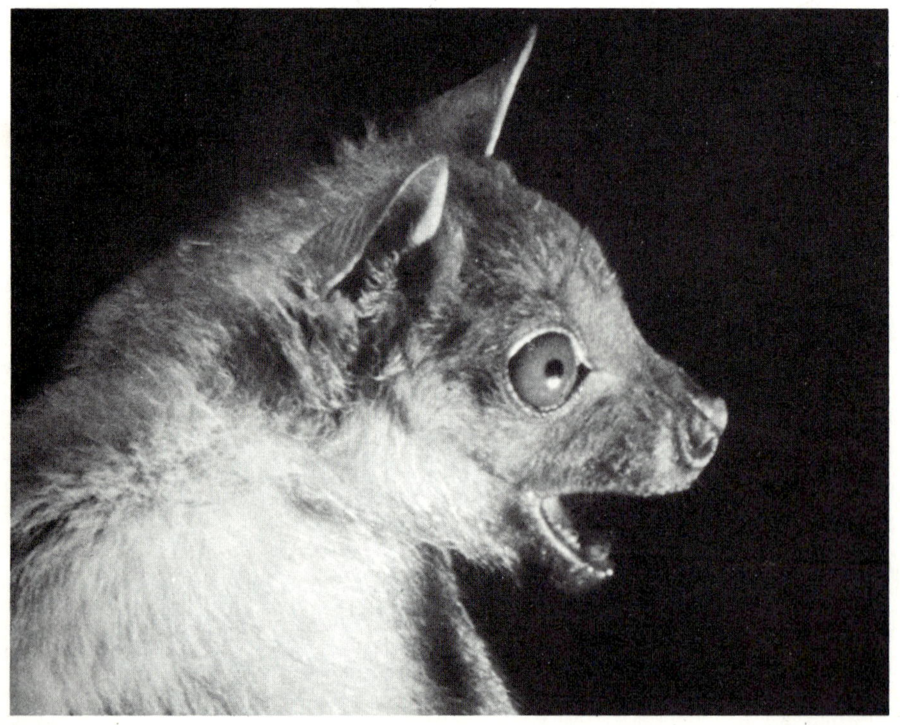

This bat looks different to different people.
Cynopterus is called variously short-nosed
fruit bat, small fox-bat, or dog-faced fruit bat.

Pallid bat, *Antrozous*, has a pleasing face
framed by long, wooly fur.

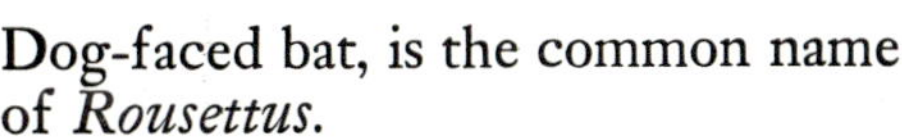

Dog-faced bat, is the common name
of *Rousettus*.

The lump-nosed bat, *Plecotus*, is not the
towering, hairy apparition it appears to be.
It weighs about 15 grams and its diet
consists mainly of moths.

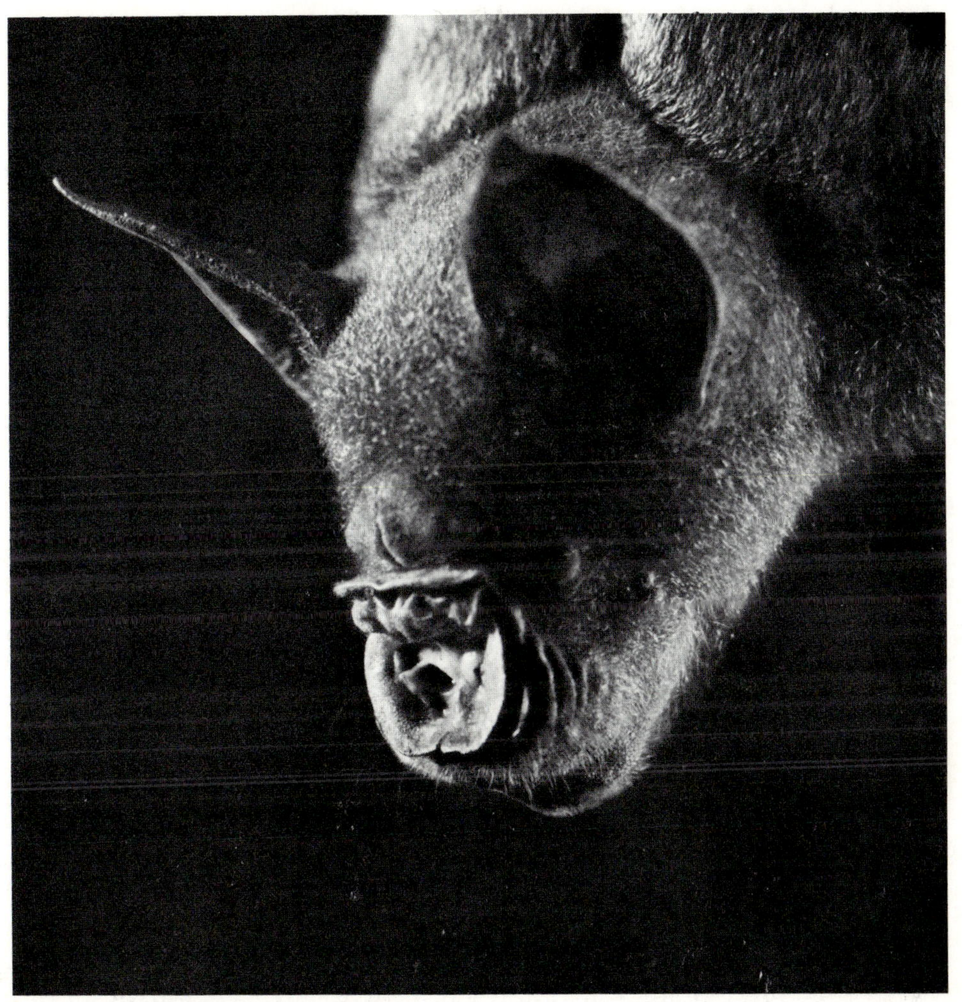

The leaf-nosed bat, *Hipposideros,*
has a horseshoe-shaped structure around
the nostrils. It is a necessary device
to emit ultrasonic sounds when the bat goes
insect hunting.

Jamaican flower bat, *Phyllonycteris aphylla*, with its silky, silvery fur and piglike snout, has the look of a stuffed toy.

The fishing bat, *Noctilio*, has a bright orange face and resembles an animal cartoon character.

Like a mythical giant, the small velvety, free-tailed bat,
Molossus, is resting on a flat rock. It sets out,
often before sundown, to hunt insects.

Wings and Flight

Dog-faced bat, *Rousettus*, has its wings partly folded. The back of its hand, with five fingers, looks nearly human. The thumb is free, the membrane of the wing is attached to the other four fingers.

Big-eared bat, *Macrotus*, in flight.
The membrane of the bat extends from its body to the tips
of its fingers, legs, and tail.

Giant African leaf-nosed bat, spreads
its wings before flight. As the bat at left closes its
wings, the loose skin shrinks together.

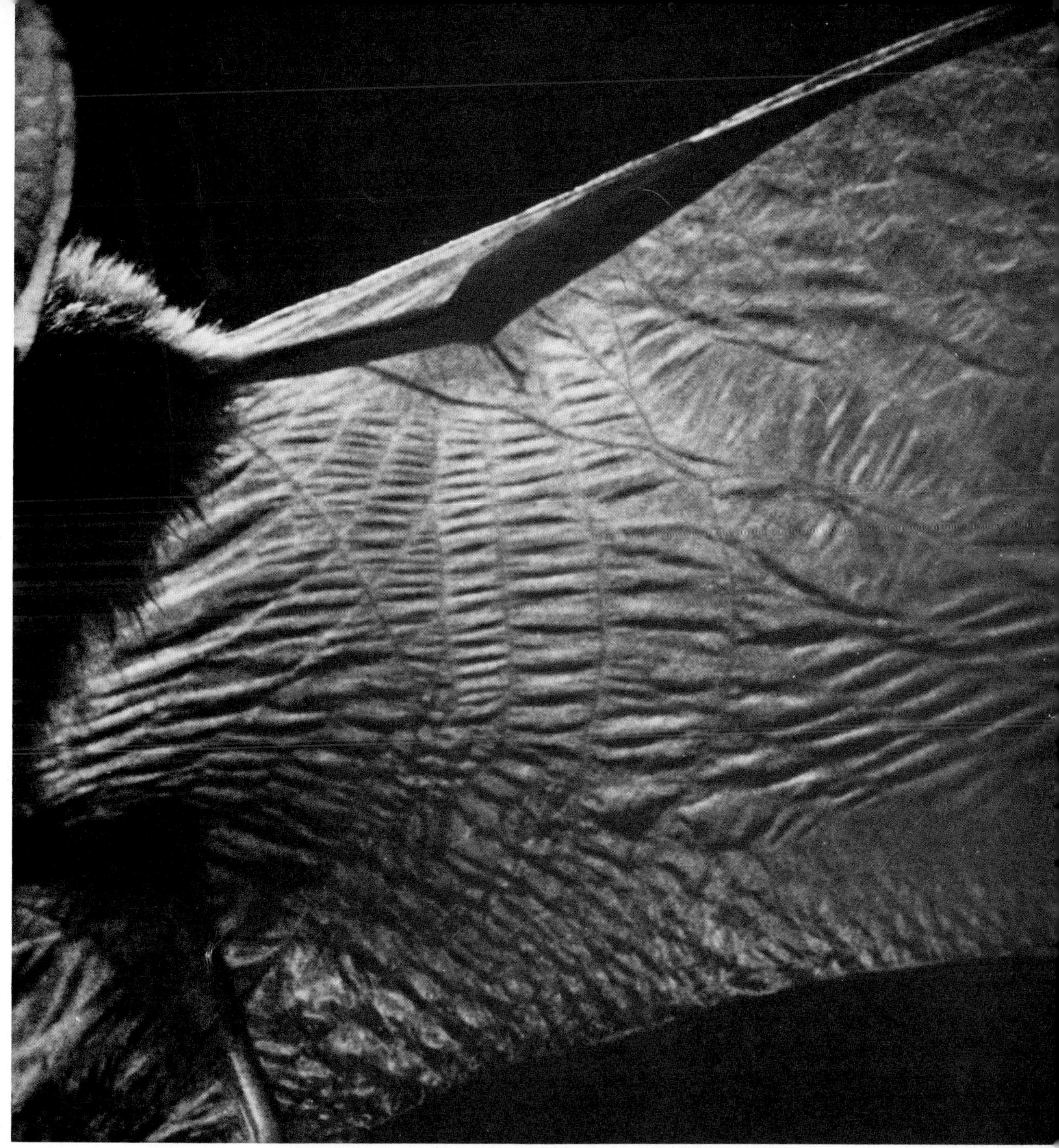

Wings of the lump-nosed bat, *Plecotus,* enlarged. Its
ingenious structure is unique.
Little wrinkles in the skin open and fold
individually, making it extremely elastic. Between
two layers of thin skin are numerous blood vessels
and nerves.

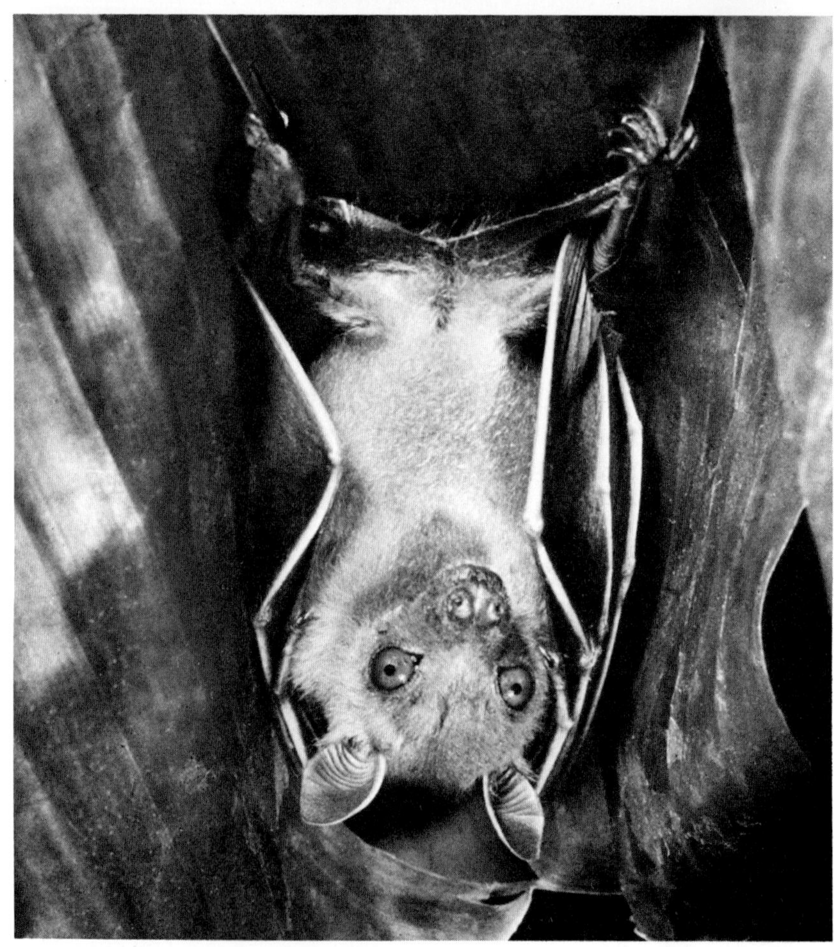

Landing on a banana leaf, the Malaysian
short-nosed fruit bat prepares to roost.

The wings of the free-tailed bat,
Tadarida macrotis, are folded
completely out of sight.

Hanging securely, the bat covers itself
with its wings before going to sleep.

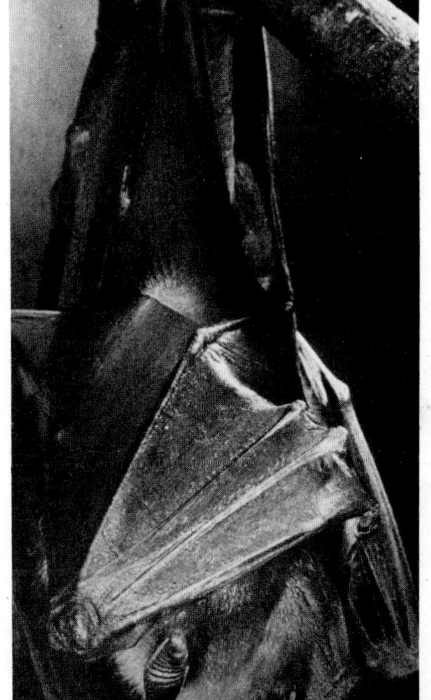

A flying fox uses wings to cover its head.

The wing of *Rousettus* is like
an umberella turned inside out
when the bat makes a turn.

Some small bats such as *Macrotus*
can fly close to the ground,
between shrubs, making fast
turns in tight places.

Its stomach well filled,
a flying fox is coming back
to roost.

Jamaican nectar-feeder, emitting
ultrasonic cries, hovers over
a leaf. Its fingers bend in
different directions.

Bats Swim, Walk, Climb, and Jump

The flying fox swims as well as many other mammals do.
With fast strokes, the bat makes its way across water
till it reaches the shore.

If the big-eared bat accidentally falls into water,
it can rise and take off swiftly from the surface.

Holding on with the claws
of its thumbs, a flying fox
moves along a branch.

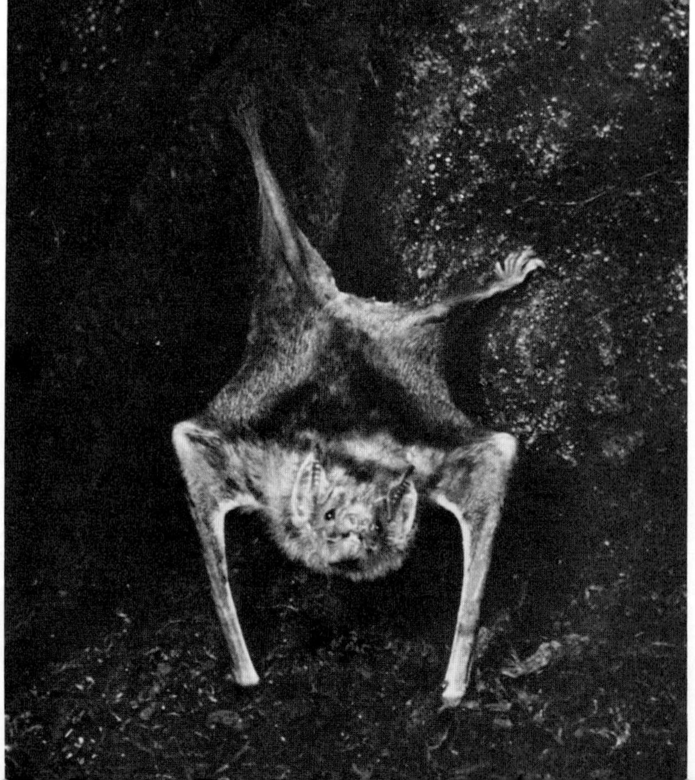

Its folded wings still
on the ground, the vampire bat
climbs up the cave wall—backward.

Free-tailed bat, *Tadarida macrotis*, sits upright, using
its thumb to investigate a possible roosting place.
Moving on a flat surface, it stops when another
bat is in its way and often backs up and walks away.

Giant African leaf-nosed bat drops from a tree branch,
spreads its wings, and takes flight.

If, by accident, it lands on the ground, the big bat is quite
helpless—it is unable to walk, crawl, or take off.

Double exposure shows the big-eared bat, *Macrotus*, in a vertical "liftoff." Although it is unable to walk, the bat can easily take off from the ground.

Two vampires were walking. One of them,
for reasons known only to itself, jumps over
its companion. No other bat can leap like a frog.

Vampires are unique among bats. They can leap forward, backward and sideways, stand, and even walk upright. Their way of life demands this agility; a clumsy bat could awaken the animal it approaches—a quick jump backward may save the bat's life.

Out of a Texas cave, a long column of insect-eating
guano bats flys to far-away feeding grounds.
They start before sundown, but it is night by the
time the tail of the column reaches its destination.
Every year, the guano bats in Texas consume between
6,000–7,000 tons of insects—a most effective
insecticide.

A Varied Diet Includes Fish, Flowers, and Scorpions

Insect eaters in flight. *Top*, California big-eared bat.
Right, Giant African leaf-nosed bat. *Bottom*, Pallid bat.

A nectar-drinking bat arrives when it is time
for the flowers to open. Finding a convenient perch
is no problem for a winged feeder.

Nectar-feeders, *Leptonycteris*, are small bats with long snouts
and very long tongues, feeding on pollen and nectar of flowers.
The night-blooming century plant is favored. Like giant
butterflies, they perch on top of the golden flower.

Hovering close to the protruding flowers of the
agave plant, the Nectar-feeder laps up the sweet
juice with its tongue.

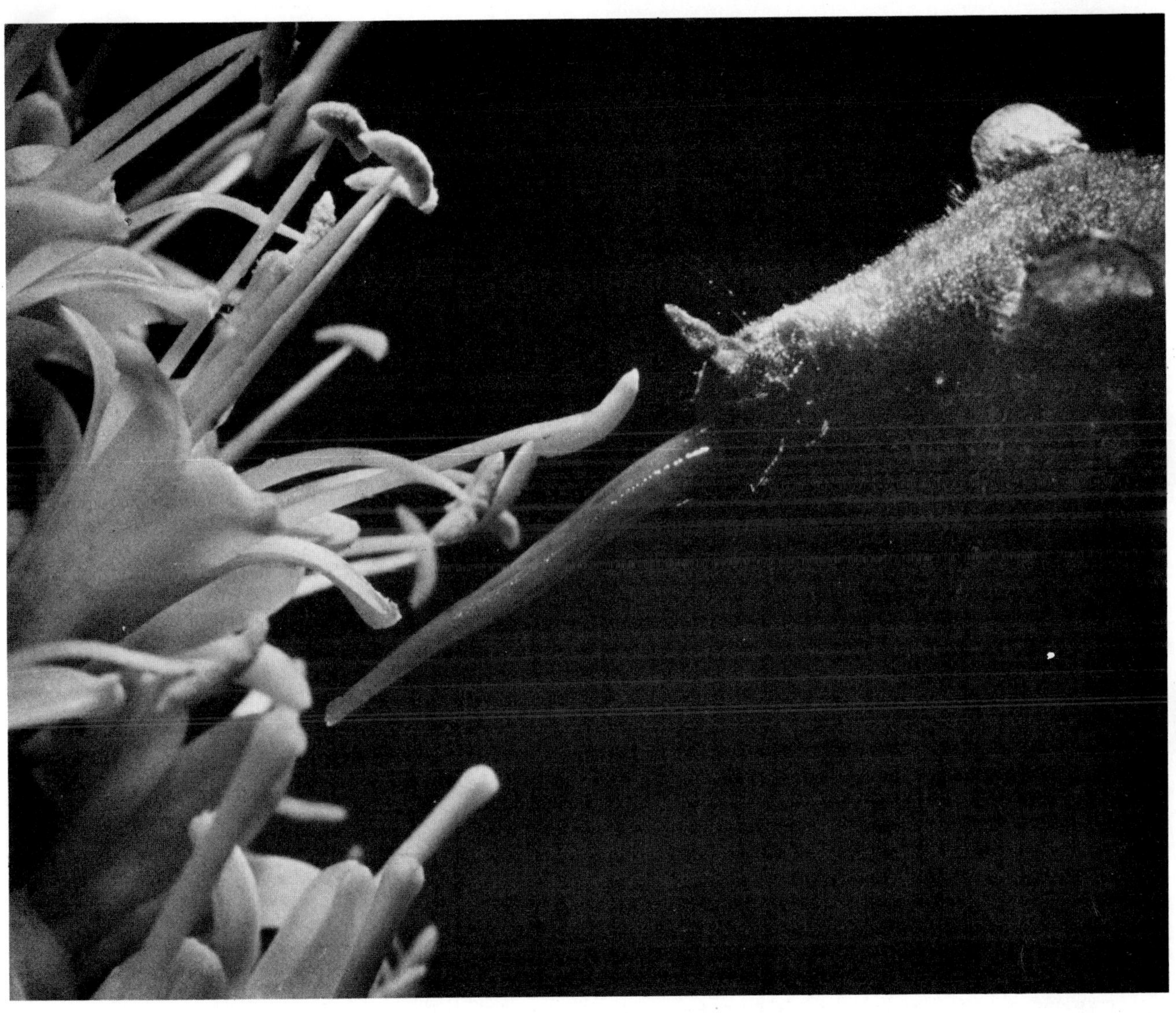

The tongue of the Jamaican Flower bat is long enough to reach
nectar in the deepest corolla. Grains of pollen often
remain on their snouts. It pollinates the flowers they
visit next. Certain plants depend only on bat pollination.

An early arriver found the cactus
flower still closed.

Hunger and determination helped the
bat to open the flower and dip in.

For only a few hours at night, the flowers of the Saguaro
cactus bloom. This is the time when nectar feeders
appear. It is often 30 miles from their home roost to the
desert cactus. They arrive very hungry and eat till their
bellies are as full and round as balloons. Sometimes, those
balloons are too heavy to fly with—then the bat takes a rest,
hanging from the stalk of the flower—till the meal is digested.

Flying foxes are fruit eaters. After a leisurely
meal, the rest of the fruit is stored in cheek pouches
for later use.

A friend tries for a bite of banana, but the eating
bat is not willing to share it.

To avoid future intrusions, the fruit
is shifted from the pouch to the mouth.

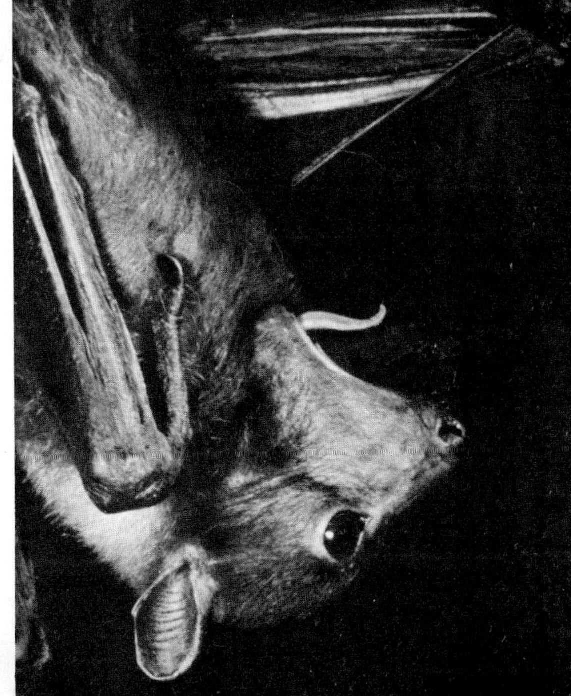

The Jamaican flower bat, *Phyllonycteris aphylla,*
is so seldom seen by people that for 75 years
it was considered to be extinct. Its name suggests
a diet of flowers and fruits. When a mango fruit
falls from a tree and splits open, the smell
attracts the bat. It has to find the broken
part to get to the pulp.

Lowering itself from a nearby branch, the bat drinks the juice and munches the pulp.

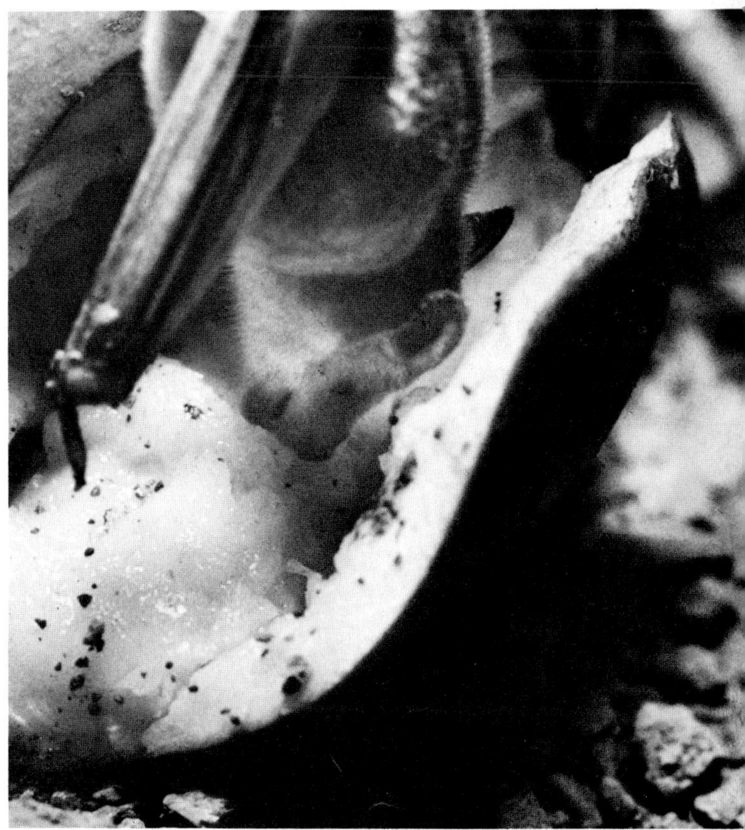

The fruit is usually not split where the bat would like to have it. Some climbing around is necessary to reach the open part.

The big-eared bat, *Macrotus*, spotted a large moth
resting on the ground. Landing close by, it observes
with obvious anticipation the oversized prey.

Small bats, like *Macrotus* have been observed
eating large moths. Sometimes, they are not hungry enough
to bother. *Macrotus*, an insect eater, uses echolocation
and sight to detect the quarry.

Hanging from a rock, *Macrotus* snatched a scorpion
from the ground. Grasshoppers, crickets, cicadas,
and caterpillars are also on the menu of this bat.
Scorpions are a favored delicacy of another insect
eater, the pallid bat.

Roosting securely, the bat proceeds
to eat what is left of the scorpion.
Everything is eaten except the tail.
Some years ago, scientists were
baffled to find small mountains of
scorpion tails beside rocks, in the desert.
The mystery was solved when bat roosts
were discovered nearby.

Disabling the scorpion with a quick
bite, the bat backs up carrying
the multilegged prey to a more
comfortable spot.

Noctilio is an adept fishcatcher. Mouth wide open,
emitting ultrasonic cries, it flys low over water.
When a fish even slightly breaks the surface, the bat
swoops down. Long toe claws gaff the fish and bring it
up to the mouth. Holding the fish with its teeth,
Noctilio returns to its roost to eat.

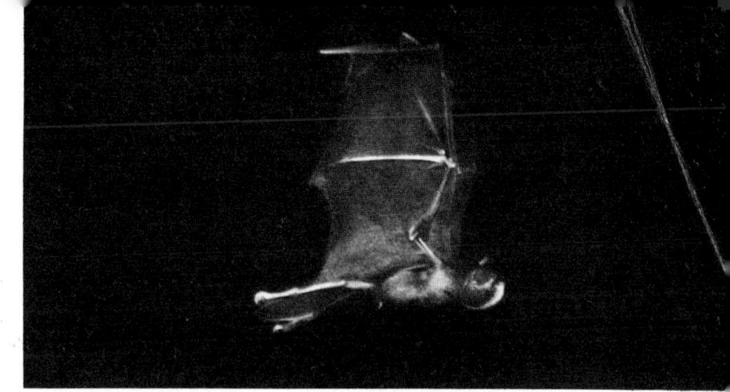

The false vampire, *Vampyrum spectrum,* brings a mouse
to its roost. The largest bat in the New World, with a
wingspan well over two feet, the false vampire is
carnivorous. Its diet includes birds, rodents, and
smaller bats. Over 200 years ago, a scientist,
Linnaeus, called it a vampire, assuming incorrectly that this
bat drinks blood.

The vampire, a small bat, eats no food
except blood. A unique, tubular stomach is adapted to
a liquid diet. Two sharp, incisor teeth are used to make
small, shallow cuts in the "blood donor's" skin.
A curved tongue, placed over the deep groove in the lower
lip, directs the flow of blood into the bat's mouth.
There are no vampire bats in the United States.

A cluster of mustache bats, *Pteronotus parnellii.*
Awakened by some disturbance, big mouths wide open,
they emit ultrasonic sounds to "find" the intruder.

Way of Life

High up on a tree is a "camp" of flying foxes.
Arriving to roost in the morning, they push, bicker,
and fight for space. Their voices can be heard
a mile away. Settling down at last, they spend the
rest of the day sleeping, cleaning themselves, and
moving along the branches; but even then, some
loud arguments can be heard. The camp is never quiet.

Jamaican flower bat sleeps,
holding on to the tree with its
toe claws.

The yellow-shouldered bat,
Sturnira, a small
fruit bat, roosts in different
locations. Two of them found
shelter in a bunch of bananas.

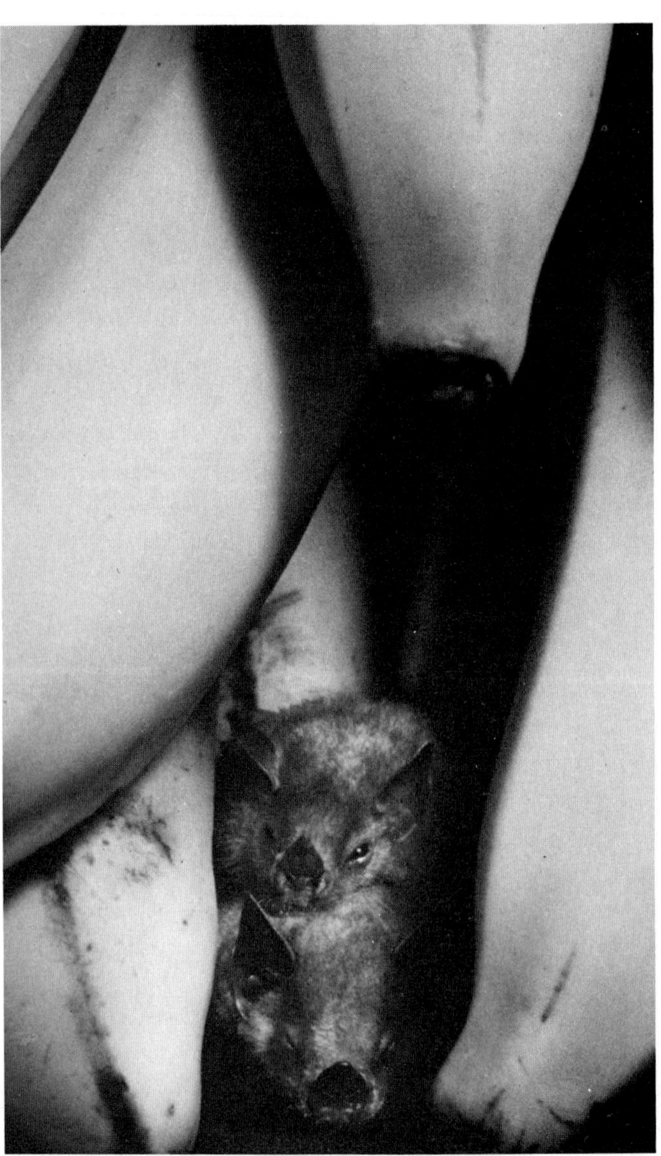

Epaulette fruit bat
from Africa often
roosts alone in well-
lighted sheds, amid
foliage or in big hollow
trees.

1. Sad story in the life of a flying fox.
   Something made the group mad enough to attack
   a young bat. Horrified, it faced the aggressors. There was no
   escape—one bat held its leg firm with a
   thumb claw.

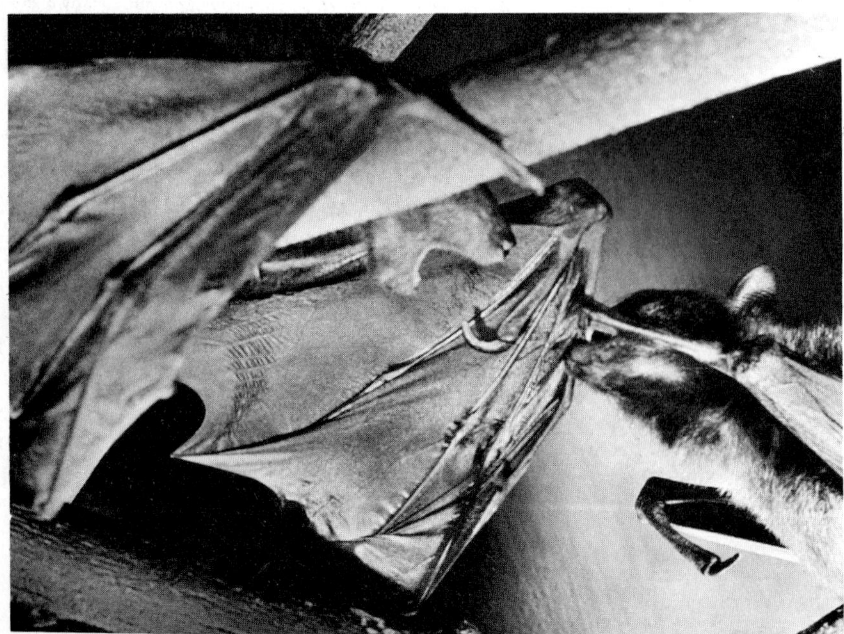

2. Loud cries did not stop
   another attacker from
   biting its wing.

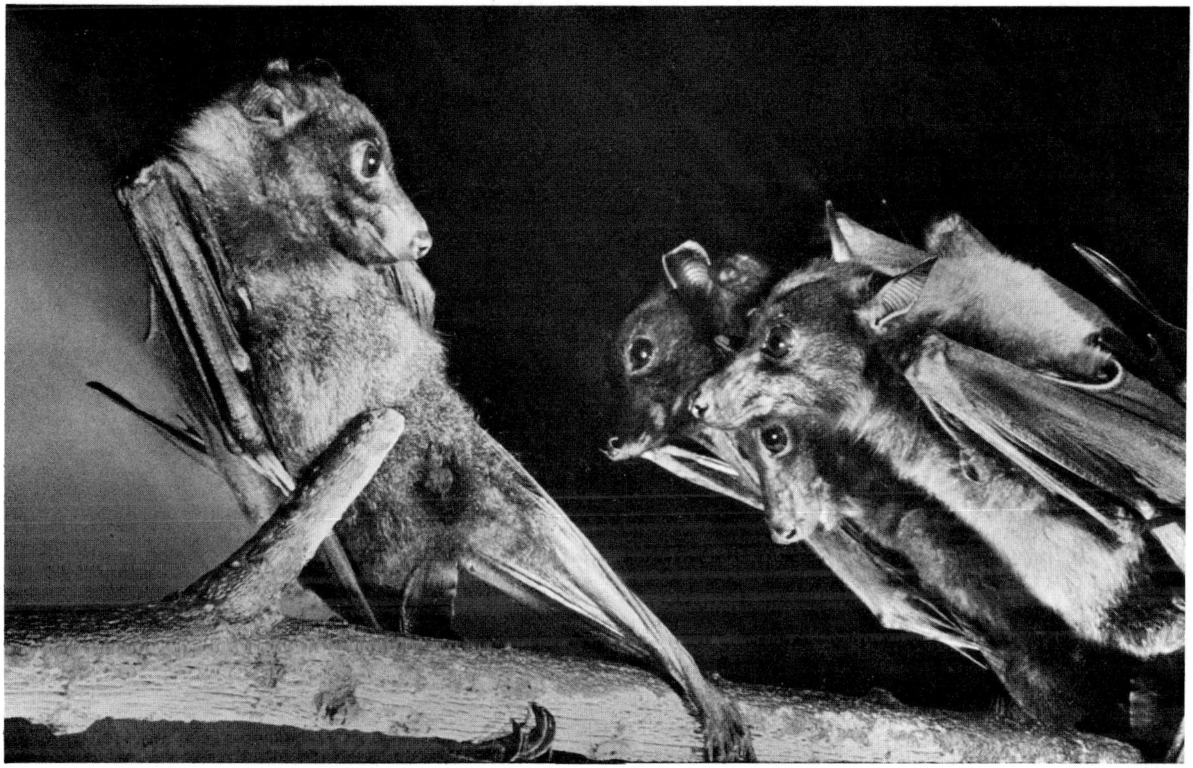

3. Trying to keep the injured wing away from the advancing
   tormentors, the frightened bat glares at the enemy.

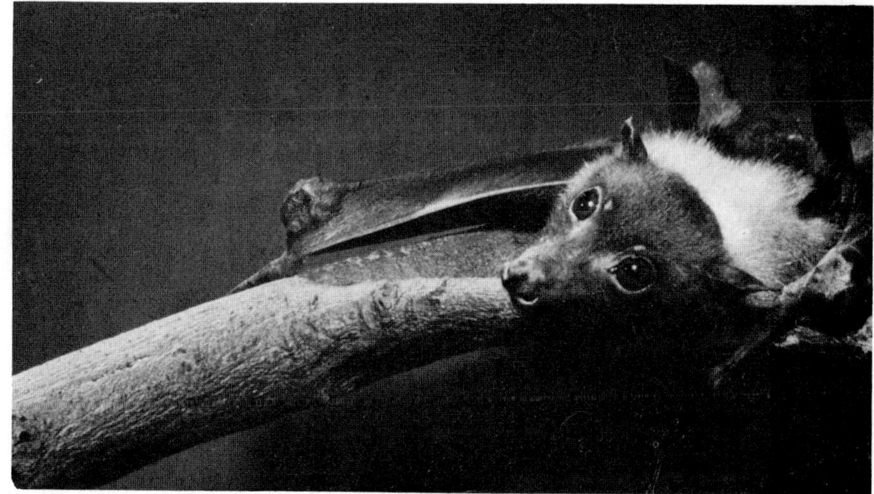

4. When the group gave up,
   the young bat fled to the
   far end of a branch, still
   shaken by its painful ordeal.
   Pictures 1, 2, and 3 are printed
   upside down for human convenience.

The African leaf-nosed bats do not roost close
to each other, always keeping a distance between themselves.
When a bat moves near a neighbor, a sham fight starts.
They threaten and shove, even "yell"—but the sounds are
mostly ultrasonic.

When the fight gets to be rough, the best solution is to give in and move apart. That is what they usually do.

With special care, the bat
cleans its nose leaf.

The ear is cleaned
with a foot.

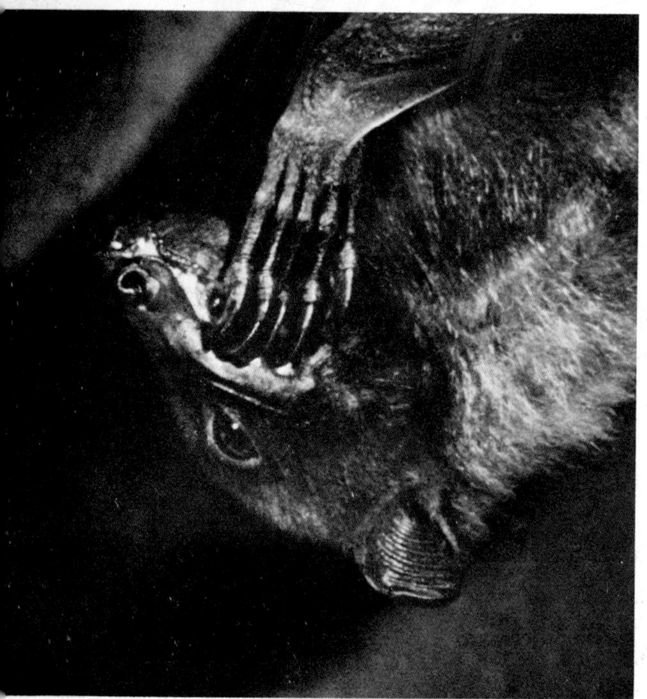

Claws are used instead
of a toothbrush.

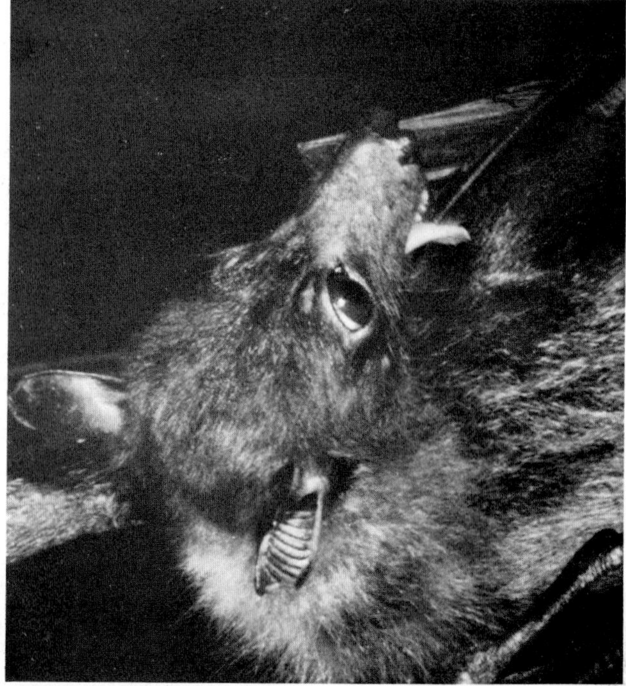

The tongue can reach most
of the furry body.

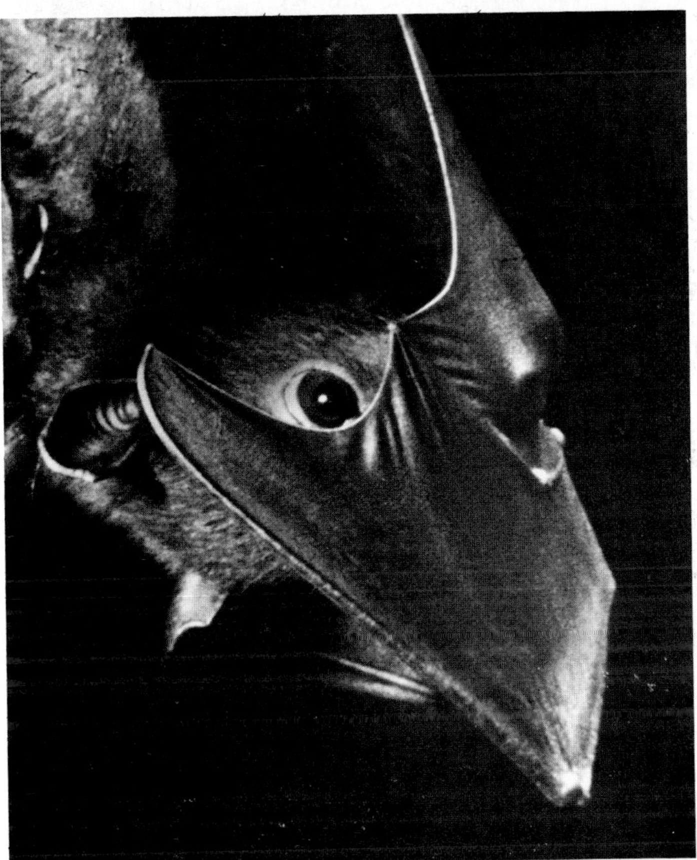

Cleaning is an important part of bats' lives. They do it when awakened, before eating, after eating, before they go to sleep, and whenever they have time. Wings are especially important—a bat's life depends on their condition.

To avoid getting soiled, a bat will twist its body or hang right side up as it relieves itself.

A Maternity Cave

Each year, 100 million pregnant free-tailed bats, *Tadarida brasiliensis*, fly from Mexico to caves in Texas to give birth to their young. Twenty million came to the Bracken Cave. In the afternoon, mother bats start insect hunting. They do not all leave at once but stagger their exits in groups of several million at a time. Regrouping in the air, they fly in different directions within a radius of 50 miles.

The inside of the Bracken Cave is covered with
baby bats. The Mexican free-tailed or
guano bats leave the blind newborns
hanging on the rocky walls. The naked young
babies cling to each other in large, tight
clusters. If one baby is pulled off the wall
a whole string of babies may follow.

When the mothers return—loaded with milk—they
are "attacked" by hungry babies. The guano bat seems
not to look necessarily for her own young, but will
nurse many babies as long as her milk supply
lasts. Above, one mother is covered
with hungry babies. The second mother just landed
to nurse.

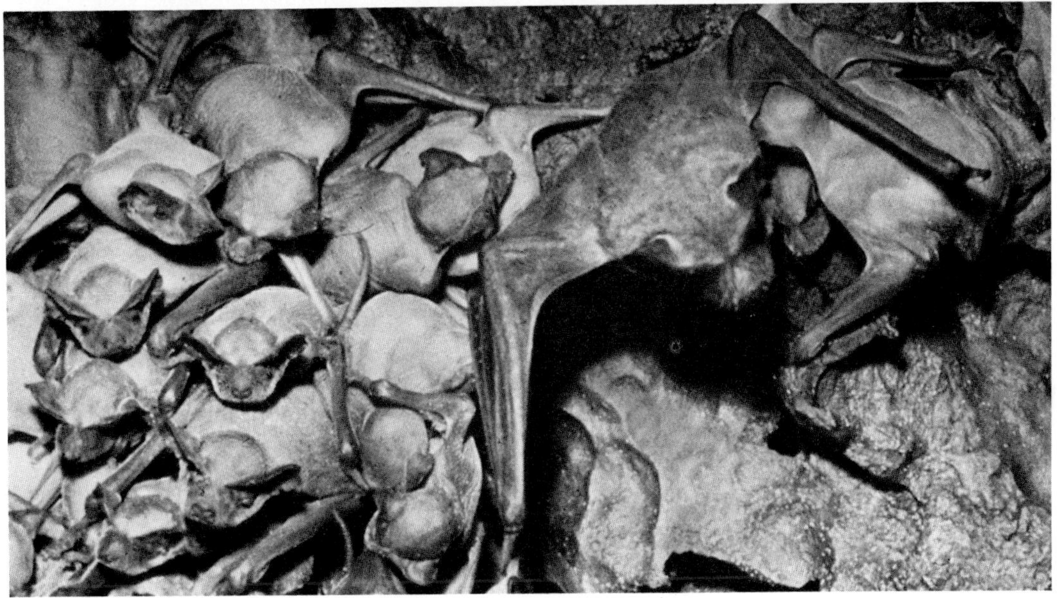

The guano babies have different temperaments;
some are more aggressive than others.
The aggressive ones get at the milk first;
the timid have to wait their turn.

These mothers never reject a
hungry baby.

Unusual and Endangered

Spotted bat, *Euderma maculatum,* is on the International List of Endangered Animals. Very little is known about this beautiful bat. White spots on its back camouflage it in nature. The large pink ears are often curled back, making the Euderma's head look surprisingly ramlike.

Coming out of a rock hollow,
the bat inspects tiny crevices
for bugs, moths, or other insects.
Whatever she finds is difficult
to record, as it is small and
rapidly eaten.

The spotted bat is an adept climber
and crawler.
It can also take off with
lightning speed into the night.

Hoary bat, *Lasiurus cinereus*, is a most unusual looking
bat in America. Covered with frosted hair, its wings partly
orange, with black-edged yellow ears, the hoary bat
is easily camouflaged on tree bark or between leaves in the
forest. It is so "invisible" in daytime and so seldom seen
by people that, in general, it is considered rare.
The hoary bat is the only bat in the Hawaiian Islands.
Nobody knows how and when it arrived. Some of them are slightly
different in color and size from the hoary bats on the
mainland. The Hawaiian hoary bat, *Lasiurus cinereus semotus*, is
on the International List of Endangered Animals.

The hoary bat is rarely
observed roosting.
Nobody would suspect the
furry cocoon hanging
between leaves to be a bat.

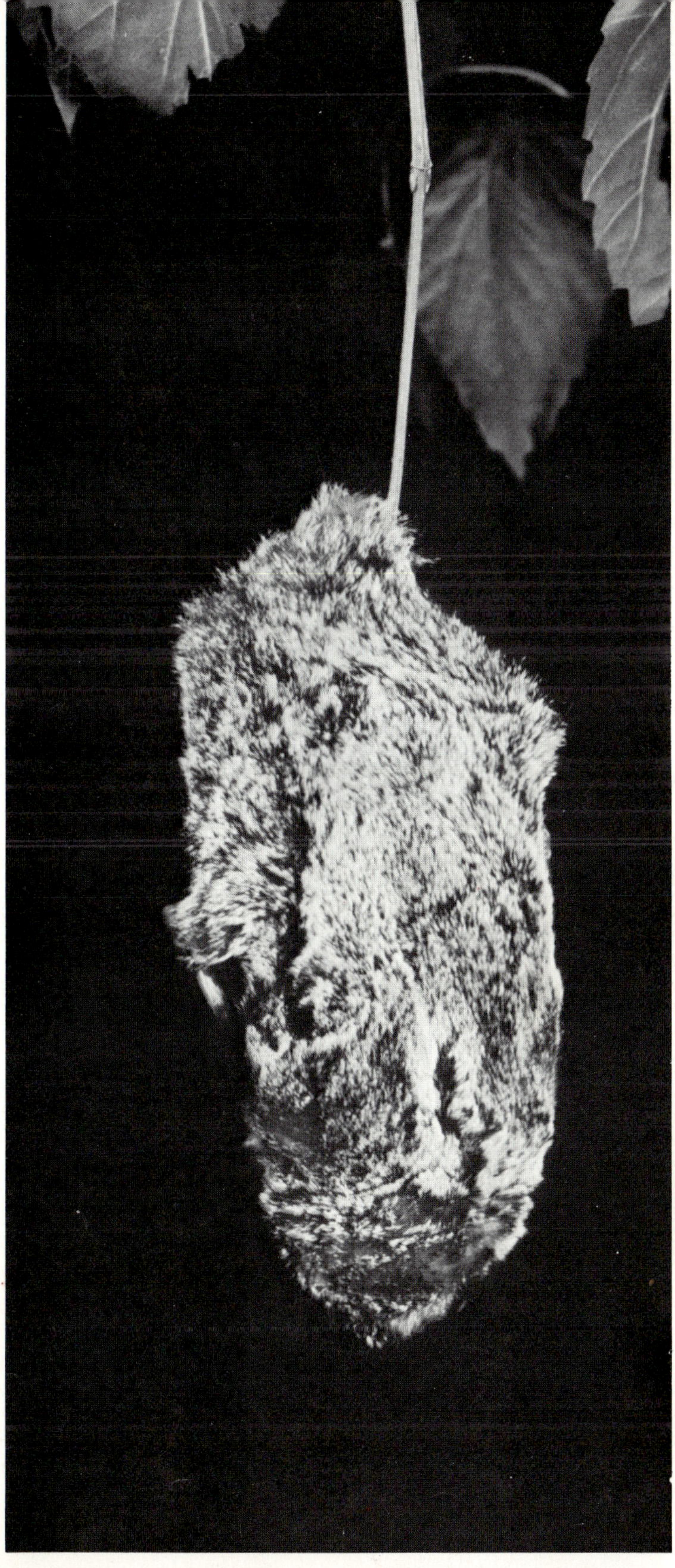

SUGGESTED READING

1 Allen, G. M. *Bats.* New York: Dover Publications, Inc., 1962.

2 Barbour, R. W., and W. H. Davis. *Bats of America.* Lexington: University Press of Kentucky, 1969.

3 Constantine, D. G. *Activity Patterns of the Mexican Free-tailed Bat.* Albuquerque: University of New Mexico Press, 1967.

4 Davis, R. B., Clyde F. Herreid II, and H. L. Short. *Mexican Free-tailed Bats in Texas.* Ecological Monograph, Vol. 32, No 4, pp. 311–346.

5 Eisentraut, M. *Aus Dem Leben Der Fledermause Und Flughunde.* Jena: Veb Gustav Fischer Verlag, 1957.

6 Goodwin, G. C., and A. M. Greenhall. "A Review of the Bats of Trinidad and Tobago." *Bull. Am. Mus. Nat. Hist.,* 122: pp. 1961.

7 Greenhall, A. M. *Notes on Behavior of Captive Vampire Bats, Mammalia,* Vol. 29, Nr 4, December 1965.

8 Griffin, D. R. *Listening in the Dark.* New Haven: Yale University Press, 1958.

9 Lavine, S. A. *Wonders of the Bat World.* New York: Dodd, Mead, 1969.

10 Leen, N., and A. Novick. *The World of Bats.* New York: Holt, Rinehart and Winston, 1970.

11 Life Nature Library. *The Mammals.* New York: Time Inc., 1963.

12 Nautuschke, G. *Heimische Fledermause.* Wittenberg Lutherstadt: A. Ziemsen Verlag, 1960.

13 Peterson, R. *Silently by Night.* New York: McGraw-Hill Book Co., 1964.

14 Walker, E. P. *Mammals of the World.* Baltimore: The Johns Hopkins Press, 1968.